Goat Behavior:
A Collection of Articles

By Tamsin Cooper

Published by karmadillo Press

karmadillo Press
22705 Hwy 36
Cheshire OR 97419
USA
(541) 998-6081
www.karmadillo.com

Author: Tamsin Cooper
Editor: Cheryl K. Smith
Cover Photo: Tamsin Cooper

*****

Cover Photo:

"Reintroductions: A high-ranking doe reasserts her authority when reintroduced to herd after a long separation. The buck-like display reinforces her higher rank over the smaller doe."

Table of Contents

Introduction

This book focuses on goat behavior. There are many excellent books about health and production. Nevertheless, when I was a new goat owner, I could not find much written about behavior in goatkeeping books. Yet, behavior is such a remarkable part of the goat experience! As a beginner, I longed to understand more about why goats act as they do.

I had volunteered at Buttercups Sanctuary for Goats, England, where disparate goats had learned to live together peacefully. But when I adopted a few lone goats into my own small herd, I ran into behavior difficulties. Simultaneously, while working at a farm park, I encountered differing opinions over the care of the animals. Resolving to find out best practices, I took some animal behavior and welfare courses offered by reputed universities, then followed up with recommended textbooks. Moving on to read published research on goats, I found that a lot of new research had been coming out during these last 20 years.

This research confirms just how unique our caprine friends' nature is, and how their needs and behaviors reflect adaptations to their ancestral environment. It also supports the notions of animal sentience, emotion and communication. It ties in so well with my observations of goats, and those of other goat owners. Moreover, we can use this knowledge to improve the efficiency of our handling and management methods.

I have compiled some of this research within three chapters, which comprise the first section of this book, focusing on three areas I feel are important to goat owners and handlers: social behavior, intelligence and emotion, and accommodation. If we understand the first two, we can adapt our techniques to work harmoniously with goats, without causing them fear or stress. Accommodating their behavioral needs will improve health and productivity. We can incorporate goat-friendly methods and design into management and facilities.

Following these core texts, I have included articles that I originally wrote for *Goat Journal/Dairy Goat Journal* and other publications.

Section II expands on the social and cognitive theme by exploring the maternal/filial relationship and body language. I also promote the protection of biodiversity as a means to ensure the future health and welfare of our animals.

Finally, in section III, I include articles that I have written about recent research and the researchers who dedicate their lives to seeking evidence to support behavioral observations. Their work is important because without such evidence we are unable to assert facts about goats in husbandry guidelines.

Bearing in mind the typical behavior described in these articles, we must also remember that each goat is an individual. Whereas research is based on data from sample herds, an individual goat may vary from the trend and have his or her own preferences and idiosyncrasies. This is where sensitivity to goat body language and good observation skills come into play. Knowing goat natural history enables us to interpret behavior from a caprine point of view, with empathy, but without asserting human values. I hope that these texts inspire you to observe and understand your goats!

Tamsin Cooper
Mayenne, France
February 20, 2018

Goat Behavior

Social Behavior

Goats are very social creatures, as anyone keeping these animals will soon find out. They frequently interact with each other and their owners. Sometimes their attentions are desirable, while at other times they are not. Understanding why they behave as they do helps us to manage them effectively, handle them easily, and even train them. It also helps us to keep the herd harmonious, a feat that can be a challenge in enclosed spaces.

To understand why goats do what they do, ethologists have studied feral populations and found that they behave similarly to their wild relatives. Reviewing studies of various populations, group size varies largely from one individual to 150 or more, but small foraging groups of two to six animals are most common.[1] Shi and Dunbar noted that goats on the Scottish Isle of Rum grouped overnight in caves and then dispersed into increasingly smaller groups over the day. The longer the day, the more these groups split as they climbed the cliff face.[2] Ævarsdóttir confirmed similar behavior in extensively farmed Icelandic goats that grazed around the farmlands in the morning and split into small browsing groups over the hillside in the afternoon. The goats regrouped under shelters during rain and overnight.[3] Both studies found that males grouped with females during the breeding season, but same-sex groups were most frequent over the rest of the year. Females grouped in *hefts* (herds that stick to a familiar range) with relatives, sisters, and kids. Males also roamed together, although they were often spotted alone when seeking out females.[2, 3]

Although family ties and nutritional needs were influential in group participation, many goats were found to have preferential partners when splitting into foraging groups. The partners were not always the same age or the closest relatives, but were consistently spotted together. These results make a case for friendship bonds beyond family ties, forming cliques for reasons other than similar foraging needs.[3] Hefts in two completely different environments—one sparse and cold, the other rich, mild grassland—revealed similar grouping tendencies. Groups of about 12 animals emerged as the core clique within each heft of 20–40 animals, with shyer animals remaining on the periphery. On Rum, a new heft was formed by peripheral animals breaking away from other hefts and forming a new social group. Within the clique and on the periphery, bonded animals were noted. Although there will always be competition between animals in a social group for nutrition and prime locations, bonded animals tolerate each other's proximity.[4]

Maintaining peace within a group is difficult as the animals are competing for the same resources. Those that have evolved group living have done so because the benefits outweigh the costs. For goats, the benefits include protection from predators and the opportunity to learn from herd members. For females, grouping helps them to attract males during the rut. The cost is competition for food and mates.

Goats develop a hierarchy to decide which animals obtain priority access, without having to fight out each case. The hierarchy is defined by age, body size, and horn size.[5] When animals are similarly sized or their ranking is not clear, they use a ualized combat routine to judge horn size, weight, and strength.[6]

Shank observed feral goats of Swiss origin on Saturna Island, Canada. He described ritualized combat as a one-on-one clash of horns where opponents approach each other with the head up, neck arched, and chin in, horns pointed forward, head slightly twisted, ears up and back behind the horns, and tail held up. The combatants engage horns and push one another's head down, twisting the neck to destabilize the opponent. One combatant may rear up before the clash, but will only engage if the opponent is ready in the appropriate posture. This ritual aims to test strength rather than cause damage.

The skull, skin, and muscles are well reinforced and can withstand such impacts. Where opponents are well matched, these struggles may last for a long time, but are tiring rather than dangerous. When one goat submits, the victor adopts a buck-like sexual display.[6]

Once a hierarchy is established within the herd, subordinates will instantly submit to dominants and get out of their way. Normally just the approach of a dominant is enough, but at times dominants give warnings: stares, a thrust of the horns, or a rush at the offending goat. A rush with the head down toward the subordinate's flank causes flight.[6] If the subordinate cannot get away in time, there may be contact and a butt. These incidents are more frequent in confinement as lower ranking individuals cannot escape quickly enough.

Goats are also seen to thrash at bushes and this may be a way of working out excess frustration in a safe way. Play fighting is common, where two or more goats spar with ritualized moves, but without the intensity of real combat. Sparring is a safe way to reaffirm rank, gauge personal ability, and practice for real contests.[6]

Males join females during the breeding season. Shank describes the male's display as gobbling: the buck extends his head toward the female's perineum, flicks his tongue, utters a guttural whicker, lunges toward her flank, and paws her. The female normally obliges by urinating and he curls his lip in a characteristic *flehmen,* during which time he analyzes her urine scent for signs of her reproductive status. If she is not in heat, he leaves her alone. If she is in estrus, she wags her tail and he guards her from other males.[6]

Subordinate males may try to court the female by gobbling when the dominant male is not looking, but he warns them off with a stare, a rush, or a butt. As he mounts, she may move forward a few paces and continue eating, but when she is ready she will stand passively and lower her head. Mating arouses attention from the other males, but in a well-controlled hierarchy, the dominant keeps them at bay.

Occasionally, dominant males have been seen to lose control over the herd; all the males have piled on to the female and fighting has broken out. This has even resulted in males falling to their death off cliffs.[6]

The female chooses her male by submitting only to the one of her choice. Females generally prefer older, larger, more dominant males. She may actively court the male of choice by rubbing against him and mounting him. Females actively butt small, young males away. These younger males display fewer courtship routines in an attempt for a brief, furtive mating. As males age, they invest more time in self-urinating and longer courtship.[6] Urinating on the mouth, beard, and front quarters enhances the male's scent, which is thought to attract females, discourage competitors, and bring females into estrus.

Polled males interact less with the herd, both socially and sexually, possibly owing to their lack of natural defenses.[6]

Rudge observed that feral goat kids hide more during the first few weeks of life than those reared in captivity. The dam rejoins the herd, leaving the kids hidden, and returns to them periodically to nurse.[7] The hiding phase is variable, as goats adapt their behavior to suit the environment.

Afterwards, kids spend more time with their dam and are weaned at about four to five months. Adult males are tolerant of kids, although dams drive away the offspring of other females. Weaning, the rut, and the following year's births gradually drive off kids to seek independence, although sometimes female yearlings regroup with their mother after she gives birth. Kids naturally form peer groups of juveniles of both sexes, and spend more time in these groups as the maternal bond weakens.[1]

Goats are adaptable and, as feral studies show, alter their behavior to suit the environment. In agriculture, they have shown that they can adapt to different systems. However, captivity and management can seriously limit their natural behavior, especially where production is intensified.

Stock densities, regrouping, early maternal separation, handling, and manipulation can all cause stress within the herd by disrupting behavioral needs. Researchers are focusing on housing and cognition to determine how enclosed goats deal with their environment and form social strategies, and what we can do to promote harmony within the herd and detect issues early. Whereas out at range, animals can avoid competition by splitting off into subgroups and foraging elsewhere, in confinement, or where there are limited feeding places, those on the periphery may lose out or suffer aggression. It is important to assess goats' personal space needs and provide escape routes for subordinates to respect hierarchical roles.[8]

Icelandic goats were found to adapt well to eating mainly grass when their preferred browse of trees, shrubs, and forbs was scarce. Goats on limited range rested more and foraged less than those that could browse freely. However, does penned continually with bucks were often harassed by them, which may explain why goats prefer separate-sex groups out of season.[3]

Goats maintain an almost linear hierarchy, which is fairly stable if the group is kept constant. The largest, oldest goats with horns enjoy the top positions and maintain them with shows of aggression. Threats are more passive at pasture but aggression intensifies in the barn, where access to feed is limited. Dominants defend access to trees at pasture, but are less defensive of pasture in the winter months, when they graze less selectively. High-ranking does' kids grow more quickly and are challenged less often. Medium-ranking does have been found to produce the most milk, perhaps because they spend less energy on aggressive defense while gaining adequate access to feed.[5]

Aggression between goats increases with stocking density and when less space is available per head at the feed trough. Aggressive acts include side locking of horns, butts to the flank, and biting. As subordinates may become excluded, trough space needs to be long enough to allow all animals to eat at the same time. Goats that have grown up in the same group and bonded goats have been found to allow closer proximity at the feed rack.[9] Lactating does can adapt to larger herd sizes, as long as per capita space is not reduced; they minimize interactions to avoid provoking aggression.[10]

Goats adopt different strategies to cope with social risk in confinement. Larger animals are generally aggressively dominant, while smaller animals avoid conflict. Dominants have the first choice of feed, while avoiders eat for longer to compensate for making do with less nutritious remains. Some goats form alliances to improve their social status and gain more access to resources, and dominants have been seen to split up fights between other herd members. Passive animals avoid interaction.[11, 12] Passive behavior may not be a successful strategy for all, however; in one study of dairy goats, passives appeared seriously underweight.[11]

Females compete for access to males, and higher ranking goats enter estrus and conceive earlier, having spent more time close to the buck.[13]

Despite increased competition in smaller enclosures, goats' desire to form groups persists, as displayed by synchronization of estrus, feeding, resting, and browsing.[9] They adapt to competition by eating more quickly,[9] remotely, or opportunistically, or by aggressively guarding feed.[5] Goats have been observed to reconcile after conflict by gentle touching and resting close together.[14] Adding unknown individuals destabilizes the group and combat ensues to re-establish ranking.[9]

Leadership, however, is not dependent on rank: the more experienced, mature, and inquisitive does tend to lead the herd out to pasture. Older females act as guides in pastoral systems. A mature doe emboldens the flock and leads them to suitable plants.[9] When they flee danger, it is always a doe that takes the lead.[6]

Even under farmed conditions, motherhood instincts persist. A strong mother–kid bond is formed within the first few hours. Kids prefer to hide during the first few days or weeks, and follow their dam closely thereafter.[9] Kids learn from their dam which plants to eat.[15]

Kids start to become less reliant on their parent from five weeks, as they ingest more solid food and choose to associate in groups with other kids. However, Miranda-de la Lama and Mattiello advocate delaying separation to six or seven weeks to allow healthy psychological and behavioral development.

They also suggest regular, gentle handling from an early age to prevent fear of humans and manipulations. In general, they recommend stable social groups, avoiding regrouping or isolating animals, introducing males only during the breeding season, and allowing sufficient access to resources for all goats.[9] By respecting goats' natural patterns and tendencies in these ways, we can achieve harmony and fulfillment in our herds.

References:

1. Shackleton, D.M., and Shank, C.C. 1984. A review of the social behavior of feral and wild sheep and goats. *Journal of Animal Science* 58(2): 500.

2. Shi, J., et al. 2005. Dynamics of grouping patterns and social segregation in feral goats (*Capra hircus*) on the Isle of Rum, NW Scotland. *Mammalia* 69(2): 185–99.

3. Ævarsdóttir, H.Æ. 2014. *The secret life of Icelandic goats: activity, group structure and plant selection of the Icelandic goat.* Thesis, Iceland.

4. Stanley, C.R., and Dunbar, R.I.M. 2013. Consistent social structure and optimal clique size revealed by social network analysis of feral goats, *Capra hircus. Animal Behaviour* 85(4): 771–79.

5. Barroso, F.G., Alados, C.L., and Boza, J. 2000. Social hierarchy in the domestic goat: effect on food habits and production. *Applied Animal Behaviour Science* 69(1): 35–53.

6. Shank, C.C. 1972. Some aspects of social behaviour in a population of feral goats (*Capra hircus* L.). *Zeitschrift für Tierpsychologie* 30(5): 488–528.

7. Rudge, M.R. 1970. Mother and kid behaviour in feral goats (*Capra hircus* L.). *Zeitschrift für Tierpsychologie* 27(6): 687–92.

8. Estevez, I., Andersen, I.L., and Nævdal, E. 2007. Group size, density and social dynamics in farm animals. *Applied Animal Behaviour Science* 103(3): 185–204.

9. Miranda-de la Lama, G.C., and Mattiello, S. 2010. The importance of social behaviour for goat welfare in livestock farming. *Small Ruminant Research* 90(1): 1–10.

10. Andersen, I.L., et al. 2011. The relevance of group size on goats' social dynamics in a production environment. *Applied Animal Behaviour Science* 134(3): 136–43.

11. Miranda-de la Lama, G.C., et al. 2011. Social strategies associated with identity profiles in dairy goats. *Applied Animal Behaviour Science* 134(1–2): 48–55.

12. Pascual-Alonso, M., et al. 2013. Identity profiles based on social strategies, morphology, physiology, and cognitive abilities in goats. *Journal of Veterinary Behavior: Clinical Applications and Research* 8(6): 458–65.

13. Alvarez, L., et al. 2003. Social dominance of female goats affects their response to the male effect. *Applied Animal Behaviour Science* 84(2): 119–26.

14. Schino, G. 1998. Reconciliation in domestic goats. *Behaviour* 135(3): 343–56.

15. Glasser, T.A., et al. 2009. Breed and maternal effects on the intake of tannin-rich browse by juvenile domestic goats (*Capra hircus*). *Applied Animal Behaviour Science* 119(1–2): 71–77.

Caprine Intelligence and Emotion

What is life like from a caprine perspective? It is important to understand this in order to meet your goats' needs. As we restrict their movements with enclosures and fencing, we must make sure that they can find ways to fulfill their behavioral and physical requirements. Mental states have an important influence on health. Unrelieved or long-term stress impairs the immune system, growth, and production.[1]

As *dichromats,* goats see through eyes that are sensitive to purple, blue, and green, less so to yellow, and probably not sensitive to red.[2] As their eyes are placed on the sides of the head, they have near-panoramic vision of 320–340 degrees. They have binocular vision within 63 degrees in front of the face.[3]

Their rectangular pupils are excellent for scanning the horizon and discerning sudden movements. They see well in the far and middle distance, but rely more on smell and touch close up.

Their sense of smell is much more sensitive than that of humans, and scents are heavily used for identification and communication. A second olfactory organ, the *vomeronasal gland,* detects heavy molecules and pheromones when the goat curls up the top lip in what is known as the *flehmen reflex.* Goats can hear much higher pitches than humans.[4] This sensitivity helps to explain why goats can be distressed or alarmed by sounds that humans cannot even hear.

These acute senses help goats to survive in the wild, where they need to stay alert to predation. Goats are very aware of their surroundings and will proceed cautiously in unfamiliar circumstances. Their vision helps them to seek out forage and quickly react to the slightest movement. They use vision, hearing, and scent to identify each other and communicate socially.[5] They have scent glands near their front hooves, behind each horn, and under the tail. Messages for other goats are dispersed by rubbing, urinating, and wagging the tail. Domestication has changed goats to some extent, but these senses and communication methods still shape how goats experience the world.

Complex social lives and difficult terrain have shaped goats' minds to be curious and explorative. They learn quickly from personal experience and from observing others. They have long memories for tasks and individuals. [5] Goats can learn to identify and remember abstract symbols displayed on a computer screen in return for a reward.[5, 6] They can keep track of hidden treats when containers are moved around.[7] Abilities vary according to different personality types. Sociable goats may pay more attention to herd-mates' activities, whereas aloof types seem to learn more quickly how to find food for themselves from visual cues, such as shapes and colors.

Inquisitive goats proactively explore their environment, but they may miss subtle details that more passive individuals notice, such as the repositioning of hidden food.

Alert but passive individuals appear to pay more attention to what is going on around them.[8] When heart rate was monitored, sociable goats appeared to be less excitable than loners when at range, where they could freely associate with the herd. Mutual grooming clearly had a calming effect. Feeding was the most exciting event, followed by fighting. Grooming was the most relaxing activity, followed by scratching, then resting.[9]

Goats learn from each other and from watching people.[5, 10] They are likely to follow in our footsteps, and look to us for help if they cannot access food or other resources. In trials, goats turned to experimenters when they could not open a box of treats. They approached people who were looking at them, rather than those who were looking away. Further tests confirmed that goats seek out people's faces to gain their attention. If a person's body is turned away, they will come around the front to make sure they are seen, irrespective of where the hands are positioned. They may approach from the side (perhaps not realizing that humans' peripheral vision is not as good as theirs). They are more likely to approach a person whose face they can see and whose eyes are open. They learn to anticipate a treat when a person looks directly at them. They can understand signals from people touching or pointing to the location of food, although they do not seem to understand directional eye or head gestures given by humans.[5, 11] However, they are sensitive to the direction of another goat's gaze[12], and I have noticed my own goats signaling to me using eye and head movements.

Goats are sensitive to the body language, facial expressions, and vocal tone of herd-mates and humans. They pay more attention to negative expressions of other goats, because it is important for them to react to potential danger, and they rely on the communication of herd members.[13] Ear and tail positions give indications of whether a goat is excited, stressed, relaxed, or depressed. Ears are pricked up and forward in attentive moments, and rotated backwards in unpleasant circumstances, such as fear, pain, or discomfort. Tails are held up in positive situations.[14] A tucked-in tail and hunched posture with head lowered are characteristic of sickness.

Bleats are louder and more high-pitched when goats are excited, and more variable when they are upset. Quieter, steady, low-pitched bleats are used when goats are calm and comfortable, and these are often used to keep in touch with herd members.[14] Goats in isolation give frequent, high-pitched calls when first left alone and when they can hear herd members. They are calling the herd in an attempt to be reunited. When completely alone and unable to detect other goats, an isolated individual quickly reduces the pitch and frequency of calls, as her energy drops and the attempts fail.

When an isolated goat is quiet and resting, this does not necessarily mean that she is coping well. She may have become passive in her despair, while remaining stressed at heart.[15] Bleats also confer identity, and goats raised together as kids have been found to have their own group accent.[16]

Goats tend to hide their pain, owing to their instinct to avoid predation. It is important to recognize subtle body language and expression to catch pain and disease in the early stages. Similar facial musculature in social mammals may provide the key to understanding goat expressions. Pain and fear cause humans and many mammals to tense their facial muscles, changing the shape of jaw, nostrils, and brow.[17] Face and body language can be used as indicators when monitoring pain and providing effective relief. Routine procedures, such as disbudding and elastration, have been found to cause pain. There is an increase in body shaking and rubbing the affected area after such interventions.[18, 19]

By understanding how goats see the world, watching their body language and listening to their calls, we can gain a picture of how well they are coping with their environment. But we must be careful not to base decisions on one sign in isolation. A combination of such observations provides a useful tool in preventive medicine. We can also use these indications to identify where changes in handling and management could improve harmony, health, efficiency, and production.

References:
1. Miranda-de la Lama, G.C. and Mattiello, S. 2010. The importance of social behaviour for goat welfare in livestock farming. *Small Ruminant Research* 90(1): 1–10.

2. Jacobs, G.H., Deegan, J.F. and Neitz, J.A.Y. 1998. Photopigment basis for dichromatic color vision in cows, goats, and sheep. *Visual Neuroscience* 15(3): 581–84.

3. Heesy, C.P. 2004. On the relationship between orbit orientation and binocular visual field overlap in mammals. *The Anatomical Record* 281A(1): 1104–110.

4. Broom, D.M. and Fraser, A.F. 2015. *Domestic Animal Behaviour and Welfare*. CABI, Wallingford, UK.

5. Nawroth, C. 2017. Invited review: Socio-cognitive capacities of goats and their impact on human–animal interactions. *Small Ruminant Research* 150: 7–75.

6. Langbein, J., Nürnberg, G. and Manteuffel, G. 2004. Visual discrimination learning in dwarf goats and associated changes in heart rate and heart rate variability. *Physiology & Behavior* 82(4): 601–09.

7. Nawroth, C., von Borell, E. and Langbein, J. 2015. Object permanence in the dwarf goat (*Capra aegagrus hircus*): perseveration errors and the tracking of complex movements of hidden objects. *Applied Animal Behaviour Science* 167: 20–26.

8. Nawroth, C., Prentice, P.M. and McElligott, A.G. 2016. Individual personality differences in goats predict their performance in visual learning and non-associative cognitive tasks. *Behavioural Processes* 134: 43–53.

9. Briefer, E.F., Oxley, J.A. and McElligott, A.G. 2015. Autonomic nervous system reactivity in a free-ranging mammal: effects of dominance rank and personality. *Animal Behaviour* 110: 121–32.

10. Shrader, A.M., et al. Social information, social feeding, and competition in group-living goats (*Capra hircus*). *Behavioral Ecology* 18(1): 103–07.

11. Nawroth, C. and McElligott, A.G. 2017. Human head orientation and eye visibility as indicators of attention for goats (*Capra hircus*). *Peer J* 5: e3073.

12. Kaminski, J., et al. 2005. Domestic goats, *Capra hircus*, follow gaze direction and use social cues in an object choice task. *Animal Behaviour* 69(1):11–18.

13. Bellegarde, L.G.A., et al. 2017. Face-based perception of emotions in dairy goats. *Applied Animal Behaviour Science* 193: 51–59.

14. Briefer, E.F., Tettamanti, F. and McElligott, A.G. 2015. Emotions in goats: mapping physiological, behavioural and vocal profiles. *Animal Behaviour* 99: 131–43.

15. Siebert, K., et al. 2011. Degree of social isolation affects behavioural and vocal response patterns in dwarf goats (*Capra hircus*). *Applied Animal Behaviour Science* 131(1–2): 53–62.

16. Briefer, E.F. and McElligott, A.G. 2012. Social effects on vocal ontogeny in an ungulate, the goat, *Capra hircus*. *Animal Behaviour* 83(4): 991–1000.

17. Descovich, K.A., et al. 2017. Facial expression: an under-utilised tool for the assessment of welfare in mammals. *ALTEX* 34(3): 409–29.

18. Rault, J.L., Lay, D.C., and Marchant-Forde, J.N. 2011. Castration induced pain in pigs and other livestock. *Applied Animal Behaviour Science* 135(3): 214–25.

19. Hempstead, M.N., et al. 2017. Behavioural response of dairy goat kids to cautery disbudding. *Applied Animal Behaviour Science* 194: 42–47.

Goat-Friendly Accommodation

How wonderfully adaptable goats have proved to be! They fit in well with farming routines and locations quite different from those experienced by their ancestors.

However, rapid technological progress and pressing economic and demographic demands are changing their environments ever more quickly. We need to make sure that they can keep up with the pace and continue to thrive.

There are two ways in which we can help goats to cope with a changing world. One is through careful breeding, the other through appropriate facilities. The breeding plan should focus on genetic variety and health traits. Although not obviously the most profitable traits, they pay off in the long run by enabling more sustainable production. Biodiversity allows future generations to adapt to climatic, environmental, and management changes. In the past few decades, selective breeding has mainly focused on increasing production. As a side effect, the goats that do well on farms are those that go on to breed. Modern goats cope better with a stable routine, and are consequently more manageable if we stick to a daily schedule. This tendency could be a result of selective breeding, and researchers are studying whether domestic caprines have lost some of their ability to adjust their behavior with changing circumstances. Furthermore, we must ensure that our goats' environment meets their physical and behavioral needs. When we view life from their perspective, we can design accommodation and routines that reduce stress and promote well-being.

Space restrictions interfere with the resolution of natural hierarchical conflicts. Subordinates will always attempt to respect the personal distance of a higher-ranking individual by getting out of the way. They will not be able to do so if they get trapped in a dead end or cannot escape quickly enough. Aggression is then likely to break out.[1, 2] The common practice of buying new animals and selling excess stock disrupts the hierarchy. A new goat is unwelcome in an established herd, and their introduction invokes a contest to establish a new ranking.[3]

An existing barn or shelter can be improved by building solid partitions and elevated platforms, thereby increasing floor space and providing vulnerable herd members with places to hide and escape. A good design will ensure no dead ends and provide enough space between partitions (51 inches) to avoid goats getting trapped by aggressors. A platform height of 32 inches enables young dairy goats to jump up out of the way of dominants and to feed in peace at a higher rack. Solid partitions 43 inches long make it possible for smaller animals to feed beside a dominant herd member without being chased away. However, shorter partitions also help to reduce conflict while feeding.[1, 2]

If space dictates that goats have to feed side by side, metal palisades have been found to be the least stressful type of feed barrier. The open design enables goats to see behind them while they are eating, and to get out of the head space quickly when a dominant individual approaches. Even so, subordinates normally do not dare to feed beside dominant individuals. One solution is to distribute feed of equal quality regularly. Lower ranking goats take their turns later, or even at night. Alternatively, all the goats can be locked into feed barriers so that they all feed at the same time. In this case, blinds are required within the manger between each head to prevent nipping or butting at neighbors' heads.[4, 5]

Resting space can be divided into platforms, which double as escape ramps and resting spots. As goats prefer to lie against a wall, solid partitions increase the resting area and provide places to hide out of the sight of dominants. They can hide under platforms, or lie on top to keep an eye on their surroundings. Different levels and increased space have been shown to reduce conflict and improve conditions for subordinate herd members.[1, 6] Choice of bedding varies, with a preference for firm, thermally non-conductive surfaces, like wood, rubber, or plastic, for resting. Goats normally urinate on absorbent material, such as wood shavings or straw, and need a dry area to rest.[7]

Complications arise when new stock is introduced; an established herd does not readily accept a stranger, who is seen as competition. Goats introduced alone have been noted to suffer a high degree of stress, even after initial fighting has ceased. The new goat often hides away and is unable to gain sufficient access to feed. She may even appear calm and settled in, but her inability to meet her needs may result in health issues. Goats in a dominant position in their former herd may fare even worse than those used to a subordinate role. When new goats are introduced accompanied by familiar herd-mates, they are less stressed, and each goat receives fewer confrontations than one introduced singly. In addition, they need plenty of space when first introduced, to work out their hierarchy through combat and evasion.[3, 8]

Equally, goats suffer stress when separated from the herd, and then again when reintroduced while they reclaim their ranking. When isolated, even subordinate goats eat less, despite having the opportunity to eat undisturbed.

If a goat has to be separated, she will suffer less physically and emotionally if she can still see, hear, and have some physical contact with other herd members.[9] When individuals are moved between groups, they must again fight for their position. Reintroducing yearlings to a main herd can result in the youngsters suffering stress and deprivation. However, they have been found to suffer less if reintroduced after the adults have given birth.[10]

Goats form social bonds with long-term friends and nursery companions. Bonded goats compete less, and will often feed as close together as 20 to 40 inches, whereas goats introduced as adults need to be spaced further apart [11], unless it is possible to incorporate the features mentioned above. When selling excess stock, it is worth considering the bonds that have grown between individual animals, and avoid separation stress adding to the ordeal of settling into a new home.

Structural enrichment, such as platforms and climbing apparatus, provides opportunities for play and exercise. As domestic environments are not as challenging as wild ranging, modern domestic animals can become bored and frustrated or suffer health issues due to lack of activity or stimulation. A variety of entertainment that is frequently changed keeps animals interested and engaged.

Goats appreciate diverse kinds of vegetation, such as branches and brush, which can be hung up in different locations. They enjoy items that they can explore, climb, rub against, and butt. Rocks are ideal for climbing and keeping hoofs in good shape. Alternatively, they enjoy standing on tree stumps, logs, ramps, and platforms. Climbing structures can be constructed from simple and inexpensive materials, such as pallets, cable spools, tractor tires, and planks. Wooden posts, sticks, and brushes attached to vertical supports are appreciated for rubbing, scratching, and butting. Goats enjoy exploring different shapes and textures with their mobile lips, favoring plastic, cloth, and wooden items. Introducing items, such as plastic bowls and balls, gives them something new and safe to explore, and such toys can easily be replaced once the novelty wears off. An Internet search for "goat enrichment" brings up many wonderful ideas.

Physical activity is very important for both physical and mental health, but we must not neglect mental stimulation. Goats are very curious, and brain training helps them to develop skills to cope with life's changes. Goats enjoy new things when they feel safe to explore them and free to escape if necessary. When placed in a new scenario, they may find it hard to cope unless they learn a strategy. A variety of cognitive enrichment can help them to develop such skills.

In trials, goats provided with physical enrichment were more active in their investigation of new objects and places, while those with cognitive enrichment were more curious and explorative. The cognitive test involved learning that buttons next to certain shapes could be pressed to deliver a reward.[12] When heart rate was monitored, it was found that goats learning a cognitive test were initially stressed or excited, but relaxed once they had cracked the code.[13] When given a choice, some goats preferred to use a shape puzzle to deliver water. They tended to be the ones who made good learning progress.[14] This suggests that brain puzzles could complement goat entertainment, if well balanced with structural and physical enrichment. Research continues to investigate how cognitive training can provide mental satisfaction for goats in unchanging surroundings.

We can provide mental stimulation by providing homemade puzzles dispensing treats. Equally, climbing puzzles, such as narrow ledges and seesaws, can provide a mental as well as a physical challenge. When I first unloaded a large pile of logs in my goats' field, they initially just sniffed and nibbled the bark. After a few days, they rose to the challenge of wobbling up and over the pile, seemingly just for the fun of it. Soon they were running and playing over it with gleeful agility. Such activity also encourages healthy, playful social interaction, which helps to bond the group.

Goats are much more able to deal with life's challenges in an environment which is comfortable and stimulating, and which facilitates the easing of social tensions. A stable social life and a family upbringing are crucial for normal, healthy development and harmonious social integration. Health and production benefit from good mental and physical well-being. Sustainable production in the long term requires that we focus on the welfare and biodiversity of our animals and their descendants.

References:

1. Aschwanden, J., et al. 2009. Loose housing of small goat groups: influence of visual cover and elevated levels on feeding, resting and agonistic behaviour. *Applied Animal Behaviour Science* 119(3–4): 171–79.

2. Aschwanden, J., et al. 2009. Structural modifications at the feeding place: effects of partitions and platforms on feeding and social behaviour of goats. *Applied Animal Behaviour Science* 119(3–4): 180–92.

3. Patt, A., et al. 2012. The introduction of individual goats into small established groups has serious negative effects on the introduced goat but not on resident goats. *Applied Animal Behaviour Science* 138(1–2): 47–59.

4. Nordmann, E., et al. 2011. Feed barrier design affects behaviour and physiology in goats. *Applied Animal Behaviour Science* 133(1–2): 40–53.

5. Nordmann, E., et al. 2015. Head partitions at the feed barrier affect behaviour of goats. *Applied Animal Behaviour Science* 167: 9–19.

6. Andersen, I.L., and Bøe, K.E. 2007. Resting pattern and social interactions in goats – the impact of size and organisation of lying space. *Applied Animal Behaviour Science* 108(12): 89–103.

7. Sutherland, M.A., et al. 2017. Dairy goats prefer to use different flooring types to perform different behaviours. *Applied Animal Behaviour Science* 197: 24–31.

8. Patt, A., et al. 2013. Behavioural and physiological reactions of goats confronted with an unfamiliar group either when alone or with two

peers. *Applied Animal Behaviour Science* 146(1–4): 56–65.

9. Patt, A., et al. 2013. Factors influencing the welfare of goats in small established groups during the separation and reintegration of individuals. *Applied Animal Behaviour Science*, 144(1–2): 63–72.

10. Szabò, S., et al. 2013. Introducing young dairy goats into the adult herd after parturition reduces social stress. *Journal of Dairy Science* 96(9): 5644–55.

11. Aschwanden, J., et al. 2008. Social distances of goats at the feeding rack: Influence of the quality of social bonds, rank differences, grouping age and presence of horns. *Applied Animal Behaviour Science* 114(1–2): 116–31.

12. Oesterwind, S., et al. 2016. Impact of structural and cognitive enrichment on the learning performance, behavior and physiology of dwarf goats (*Capra aegagrus hircus*). *Applied Animal Behaviour Science* 177: 34–41.

13. Langbein, J., Nürnberg, G., and Manteuffel, G. 2004. Visual discrimination learning in dwarf goats and associated changes in heart rate and heart rate variability. *Physiology & Behavior* 82(4): 601–09.

14. Langbein, J., Siebert, K., and Nürnberg, G. 2009. On the use of an automated learning device by group-housed dwarf goats: do goats seek cognitive challenges? *Applied Animal Behaviour Science* 120(3–4): 150–58.

Behavior Matters

The Benefits of Natural Kid Rearing

Left to their own devices, our domestic goats have retained clever social strategies for survival, inherited from their wild ancestors. Goats have adapted well to our ways, but there is much wisdom to working in harmony with their natural systems, as it leads to better health and more sustainable production.

Researchers have recently been studying the complexity of social relationships between does and their young and the long-lasting bonds that they form. Discoveries of the secret lives of these most familiar animals can help us to improve our systems and management procedures. Many of these behaviors you will have seen yourself. I have found that it is useful to consider them from the perspective of goats' natural history.

Newborns are quick to get up on their feet, but they need rest, while their mother's priority is to feed herself up to provide them with milk. They hide out in the undergrowth, and she returns a few times a day for nursing. She has several ways of seeking them out.

A keen sense of smell works well close up. As she licks her kids clean after birth, she learns their individual scents and forms a strong maternal bond. But odors don't travel far. Mother and offspring must quickly learn to identify family voices. By four hours after birth, the dam can identify them from sight and sound, and by two days, from sound only. This helps if they are hidden from view in long grass. As kids grow, their bleats change.

Distinct properties of their calls vary according to age, sex, and body size.

However, the dam still remembers their individual voices, even when recordings are played back to her a year later. Kids hide out less and follow their dams more after a few days or weeks. By their mother's side, they learn which plants to eat and which to avoid. After five weeks old, they become a little more independent of their mother, and they naturally start spending more time with kids their own age. Kids form peer groups of their own accord, and start to establish long-lasting friendships. Their calls develop to resemble one another's, forming a group accent.

When growing up in a natural herd of related females and their kids, youngsters learn the subtle social skills required to fit into goat society. Constant fights are prevented by each goat knowing her place and yielding to more dominant members. From six months of age, a kid starts to negotiate her position in the ranking. She engages in ritual combat with other herd members, by locking horns and pushing, to compare her strength to theirs. Play-fighting among kids is great training for this serious adult game. As she grows, she renegotiates for a higher ranking. By knowing her place and respecting the hierarchy, she stays safe. She learns strategies for accessing food without aggression. She will avoid getting in the way of older and stronger herd members. She will seek out the best places and opportunities to find food without coming into conflict.

Female relatives form lifelong bonds. Even after weaning, which usually occurs naturally between three and six months, they retain strong friendships with their mother and nursery companions. The dam may chase her yearlings away when she next gives birth, but they frequently reconcile as her new kids join the herd. On reaching sexual maturity, males naturally disperse to seek out mates. They form a loose bachelor herd outside the breeding season. During the rut, the dominant male will find and join a female herd.

Knowledge of the delicacy of goat society highlights some possible causes of stress frequently suffered by farm animals. It is easy to forget how social bonds may affect individual animals when buying and selling livestock. It raises the question of how we may mitigate such stresses by changing our management techniques.

Animal scientists sat down to discuss the feasibility of dairy animals raising their own young during the International Society for Applied Ethology (ISAE) conference in 2015. They reviewed recent research and current practices on dairy farms. Although they focused on dairy cattle, the physiological and behavioral phenomena discussed apply equally to dairy goats.

Studies of calves raised on the cow revealed that they coped better when introduced to the milking herd. Dam-raised calves employed more effective social strategies compared to calves separated from their mothers at birth. ISAE participants agreed that the half-day contact system was less stressful for the calves before and after weaning. It encouraged calves to learn new feeding systems and to socialize with humans. Here calves are separated from dams at night, the cows are milked in the morning, and then cow and calf stay together during the day. As kids naturally form nursery groups, this system also works well for goats, and several organic dairy farms have successfully adopted this practice. Where separation is deemed necessary, researchers recommend that kids not be separated from their mothers too early, as the infant may develop behavioral problems, which will also affect growth and future production. They suggest six to seven weeks as the earliest time for maternal separation. At this time kids naturally bond with others of the same age.

Kids feel safer hiding while their mother is out of sight. Placing a box or platform in the stall and at pasture gives them this natural option to calm their own fears. When raising fully on the dam, you may find that you need to enforce weaning by three to four months old, because milkers don't dry up as quickly as their ancestors.

Fence-line methods are recommended for calves, allowing visual and tactile contact, but preventing suckling. Staged separation was also recommended by ISAE participants. Half-day separation gets youngsters used to time away from their mothers and strengthens their bonds with peers and human carers. In this way, they become prepared for eventual permanent separation.

Although there is still much to be studied as regards alternative rearing systems in large-scale production, evidence suggests that changes which respect dairy animals' social needs improve health, welfare, and productive life. In small-scale and organic production, inexpensive changes to housing and social routine can vastly improve the harmony, health, and happiness of our herds.

Sources:

Briefer, E., and McElligott, A.G. 2011. Indicators of age, body size and sex in goat kid calls revealed using the source–filter theory. *Applied Animal Behaviour Science* 133(3–4): 175–85.

Briefer, E., and McElligott, A.G. 2011. Mutual mother–offspring vocal recognition in an ungulate hider species (*Capra hircus*). *Animal Cognition* 14(4): 585–98.

Briefer, E.F., and McElligott, A.G. 2012. Social effects on vocal ontogeny in an ungulate, the goat, Capra hircus. *Animal Behaviour* 83(4): 991–1000.

Briefer, E.F., de la Torre, M.P., and McElligott, A.G. 2012. Mother goats do not forget their kids' calls. *Proceedings of the Royal Society of London B: Biological Sciences* 279(1743): 3749–55.

Glasser, T.A., et al. 2009. Breed and maternal effects on the intake of tannin-rich browse by juvenile domestic goats (*Capra hircus*). *Applied Animal Behaviour Science* 119: 71–77.

Johnsen, J.F., et al. 2016. Is rearing calves with the dam a feasible option for dairy farms?—Current and future research. *Applied Animal Behaviour Science* 181: 1–11.

Miranda-de la Lama, G.C., and Mattiello, S. 2010. The importance of social behaviour for goat welfare in livestock farming. *Small Ruminant Research* 90: 1–10.

Poindron, P., et al. 2007. Sensory and physiological determinants of maternal behavior in the goat (*Capra hircus*). *Hormones and Behavior* 52: 99–105.

Recognizing Caprine Body Language and Facial Expressions

Do goats express their feelings through facial expressions? And do they recognize ours? Animal behavior researchers are busy finding out.

Goats give and respond to facial expressions, researchers are discovering. They can pick up social signals from companions and herd-mates through body language, bleating, and also more subtle expressions, such as tension in the facial muscles. Last year, Scottish and French scientists found that goats paid more attention to photographs of herd-mates showing negative expressions (in response to an unpleasant sensation) than to herd-mates looking relaxed (during a grooming session). This demonstrates that they recognize feelings conveyed by their companions' faces.

We are so used to communicating through words and expressions; little do we realize our farmyard friends may use systems similar to ours. In fact, facial expression is a hot topic among animal welfare researchers as a potential key to understanding what livestock need for optimum health and welfare. Emotional expression is both a communicative gesture and a display of inner feelings. Mammals have similar facial muscles, which are affected by emotion in similar ways: tension in stressful, painful, and other negative circumstances; relaxation at calm moments; protection of eyes and ears during danger; and movement of eyes, ears, and nostrils to capture important input.

We can generalize that wide-open eyes revealing whites indicate a negative state of mind, normally fear or stress. Eyelids are retracted to improve peripheral vision, so increasing vigilance and readiness to react to danger. Whites of the eyes are revealed as eyeballs move around, checking for signs of danger. Ears swivel around to pinpoint the direction of potential threats. Surprise and uncertainty are marked by ears pointing in different directions. These are all good defense mechanisms to protect the animal from danger. However, exposure to too many frightening events is not good for your herd's health or peace of mind. Continual stress lowers the immune system and reduces growth and yield.

Fear and other negative emotions, such as pain and anger, are commonly accompanied by tension in the muscles, which changes the shape of the face. Tension may be seen around the eyes, nostrils, and in the jaw and lips.

How could facial expression help us spot negative reactions in our goats? I'm sure you've seen a lame goat suddenly burst away energetically as soon as you try to catch her. Your three-legged goat is suddenly running fine on all fours. You may feel she can't be in that much pain if she can run like that. Perhaps you wonder if she is putting on the limp. Actually it is likely to be the other way round: she is suppressing her pain reaction to avoid being caught. You may only wish to give her aid but, in her mind, being caught is a dangerous risk.

Before domestication, farm animals had already adapted their behavior to avoid predators. They tend to hide the effect of pain in their movements, not wishing to attract attention. They protect themselves from any circumstance that might cause them further pain or damage, including our interventions, as they don't realize we are trying to help them. This means that an injured or sick goat might spring into action and act perfectly well as soon as you try to catch her. However, psychologists believe facial expressions are not as readily hidden, even for humans. Animals appear to have less control over facial expressions than other postures and movements. This opens up a promising path to evaluating hidden animal pain through observing facial changes.

Many mammalian species have similar pain expressions, which makes it easier for us to recognize them. Pain expressions have been successfully defined for sheep, cattle, and horses. Similar expressions can be seen in goats during pain and illness. A sick goat may lay back her ears or hang them low, eyes may be semi-closed, jaw and nasal muscles tense, lips tight or pouting.

Faces don't just help with the negative. Relaxed facial muscles indicate positive emotions are in play. Relaxation and positive states of mind are important for goats to get the rest they need, cope better with any changes and fight disease. A goat that is being groomed droops her ears as she relaxes. Facial muscles go slack and the lower lip may loosen.

As social animals, friendly interactions are important for goats, and relaxed faces may indicate amicable intentions. During play, postures and expressions that imitate aggression are often adopted, so it is harder to gauge the seriousness of interactions. However friendly matches tend to be less intense, more ritualistic and with frequent pauses for gentle gestures, such as mouth or horn sniffing.

Goats also use their faces to signal their intent. Once a hierarchy is settled, a dominant goat will simply warn, rather than attack, by lowering her head with her ears high up and rotated towards the side or back. She'll dip her head towards an underling she wishes to move out of her way, gesturing with her horns. At close quarters, she may add stronger signals such as a grunt, flared nostrils and raised hackles. When the underling submits, she shows a fearful face, with ears laid back, and moves quickly away. She may utter a quiet moan of acquiescence.

Minimal signaling should maintain the status quo and avoid painful encounters. However, in confined spaces, like within a shelter, aggression can break out. Careful design can provide escape routes and hiding places to diffuse such encounters. Where dominant animals defend food or water, subordinates may not get enough of the right nutrition. Continual clashes also cause social stress with its detrimental effect on health and production.

Behavior monitoring can help us to design our housing to restore harmony.

Facial expression has good potential to tap into the inner feelings of our animals, but there are limitations. Many facial changes are common to different emotions. Without context and other observations we may incorrectly interpret some expressions. Pain, fear, and anger produce many common facial signs. Mock aggressive faces are often worn at play. In addition, expressions might vary between individuals. I have one goat who pouts during grooming sessions—a sign often associated with pain—but she is clearly enjoying it and wanting more!

Researchers have found sleeping, sedated or anesthetized animals may show pain expressions even though they are unlikely to be feeling anything. So facial expressions should not be used alone, but as one of many clues as to how an animal is feeling. Postural, behavioral and clinical indicators are also required for veterinary diagnosis. However, pain may not always be visually apparent in chronic cases. Sadly, chronic, subclinical disease seriously affects welfare and productivity.

Facial expressions can be fleeting and might be missed unless time is spent with your animals. The excitement of human interaction could temporarily mask or disrupt the expression. Spending time with your goats should allow their behavior to return to normal and for you to observe their body language.

Although scientific mapping of caprine expression is currently incomplete, evidence for ear positions can be found in the French and British studies: ears are positioned backward more often in negative situations, hanging down while relaxed during grooming, and forward when excited, alert or interested. Knowledge of facial expression, along with other behavioral signs, shows promise of providing diagnostic tools for the early detection of health issues as well as indicating if improvements need to be made in our handling and management systems.

Originally published as "Written on Their Faces" in the January/February 2018 issue of Goat Journal *and on countrysidenetwork.com.*

Sources:

Bellegarde, L.G., et al. 2017. Face-based perception of emotions in dairy goats. *Applied Animal Behaviour Science* 193: 51–59.

Briefer, E.F., Tettamanti, F., and McElligott, A.G., 2015. Emotions in goats: mapping physiological, behavioural and vocal profiles. *Animal Behaviour* 99: 131–43.

Descovich, K.A., et al. 2017. Facial expression: An under-utilised tool for the assessment of welfare in mammals. *ALTEX, 34*(3): 409.

Nawroth, C. 2017. Invited review: Socio-cognitive capacities of goats and their impact on human–animal interactions. *Small Ruminant Research* 150: 70–75.

Protecting Livestock Biodiversity

Many a dairy goat farmer may envy the progress of
Holstein cattle that have doubled milk production
over the last 40 years. However, looking closely,
improvements in productivity have come at a heavy
price of increased health issues and nutritional
demands. Furthermore, conservationists warn that
dwindling genetic diversity threatens the future of
farming, as animals become ill-equipped to adapt to
changing conditions or new diseases. The United
Nations are so concerned that over 100 countries are
already signed up to monitoring genealogies and
changing breeding objectives.

Since domestication, farm animals gradually
adapted to local conditions and became hardy
beasts, resistant to local diseases and well adapted
to the regional climate. Only within the last 250
years have breeders favored physical qualities that
led to established breeds. Within the last 60 years,
our improving technology has enabled us to
concentrate on production traits such as yield and
content of protein and butterfat. However, such
focus on a few traits in dairy cows has inadvertently
brought with it an increase in infertility and
production diseases. The consequences are partly
genetic, partly due to the stress imposed on a cow's
body by her high yield, and partly because of
increased indoor housing. Cows and their farmers
now struggle with mastitis, lameness, metabolic and
reproductive issues, and diminishing lifetime

profits. Consequently, breeding indexes now increasingly include health and fertility traits.

Agricultural researcher, Wendy Mercedes Rauw, studied the effects of genetic selection for yield at the Agricultural University of Norway and concluded that "when a population is genetically driven towards high production … less resources will be left to respond adequately to other demands like coping with stressors". As the cow puts all her energy into producing milk, she has less available for maintaining her health and coping with changes or problems in the environment. Indeed, Holstein milkers need high levels of feed and care and minimal stress to produce well and stay healthy. They would not be able to live a pastoral life. Nordic countries were the first to include health and reproduction objectives in their breeding plans.

Looking then at the major chèvre producer, France, I was surprised to see that mastitis resistance has only recently been incorporated into goat breeding indexes. Until now yield, protein and butterfat content and udder conformation have been the only traits documented. The high use of artificial insemination (AI) in large-scale commercial production has led to high-yielding Saanen and French Alpine does with similar physical traits. Conservation biologists' examination of the mitochondrial DNA of dairy breeds has shown a narrowing of genetic diversity in all production breeds due to the focus on high yield.

This has caused alarm in the Food and Agriculture Organization of the United Nations (FAO), which has produced two reports on the State of the World's Animal Genetic Resources for Food and Agriculture with the co-operation of 129 countries. In 2007, the FAO devised a global plan to halt the erosion of agricultural biodiversity which 109 countries adopted. By 2020 each nation should have a strategy; research and training is continuing worldwide. Goats are one of the five main species whose genetic resources are being studied.

Genetic diversity in livestock is a reservoir of traits that enables farmers to improve their stock and allows animals to adapt to changing conditions. "Genetic diversity is a prerequisite for adaptation in the face of future challenges", says FAO Director General José Graziano da Silva. As changes occur in climate, diseases, and the availability of land and resources, alternative genes allow animals to adapt.

Our past practices have led to this diversity dwindling due to various factors: the selection of similar traits for commercial gain, the spread of popular breeds worldwide, the overuse of AI (few males siring each generation), and inadvertent inbreeding through lack of family records, herd isolation, or by closing herds to protect against spread of disease.

Local heritage breeds are a source of diversity and are well adapted to regional conditions. Within the area where they have settled they have good disease resistance and are suited to the climate. Sadly, the demands of commerce have led to abandoning small-scale production from moderate-yielding animals in favor of high-yielding commercial breeds. Even where heritage breeds have been kept, dilution of the gene pool has occurred due to cross-breeding with popular production breeds. Short term, these measures have improved profitability. However, production breeds have often been developed in a foreign environment and fare poorly in the area where the landrace would have thrived. In France, the hardy French Alpine may thrive in the mountains of Savoie, but she is poorly equipped for the damp weather of the northern pastures where she suffers from parasites and respiratory diseases. This has led to Alpines being farmed indoors with consequent management and welfare issues, while the hardy landrace, Chèvre des Fossés, has brushed extinction and has only recently been recognized and protected.

France has recognized that eight of ten local breeds are at risk, but at least the genetic resource is still there to save. France's response to the FAO plan is to lead the EU initiative investigating how Moroccan goats adapt to a changeable environment, by studying the genomes of wild and traditional goats in Iran, where goats were first domesticated. They hope to find a rich resource of biodiversity. "We are dealing with a pressing conservation need", says Pierre Taberlet, project coordinator, "When a few animals are providing sperm to many, then vital genes are lost generation by generation. In a few decades, we might lose most of the highly valuable genetic resources that humanity has gradually selected over the past 10,000 years." In addition, France's agricultural department INRA and breeding authority CAPGENES are implementing a scheme to document the genealogies of all goats used for commercial production and calculate their effective population, common ancestors, and percentage of inbreeding. The aim is to control these figures and freeze the genetic erosion. They also register and provide financial assistance to local heritage breeders.

Taberlet recommends furthermore to protect the wild ancestor and restore the diversity within industrial breeds. He urges schemes to market products from lower yielding breeds with prices to reflect the costs of production. He warns, "If we lose the genetic resources now, they may be gone forever." Ecologist Stéphane Joost recommends, "Farmers should keep their local, well-adapted breeds". They may be less productive short term, but they are the wiser choice in the long run.

In an effort to safe their endangered landrace goat, Researchers at Trinity College Dublin, Ireland, examined modern dairy goats plus ferals from two populations in Ireland and compared their genetic sequences to those of historic taxidermy samples of indigenous "Old Goat" breeds. The dairy goats had little in common with historical local breed, being closely related to modern breeds of Swiss origin. Feral goats at The Burren, County Clare, were also found to have strong similarities to European samples. However, ferals at Mulranny, County Mayo, were closely related to historic and extinct samples from Scotland and Ireland, with links to old Polish and Norwegian breeds. This connection suggests inheritance from landrace animals adapted to the Irish climate, landscape and local conditions.

Trinity College Dublin's study was published in February 2017. One of the lead researchers, Valeria Mattiangeli, said: "This highlights the impact that transportation and mass importation of continental breeds has had on Ireland's goat populations, and underlines how selective breeding for agricultural purposes can impact the genetic diversity of animals."

Seán Carolan of the Old Irish Goat Society, who is a co-author of the article, said: "We hope this study will play a key role in saving what was and still is a diminutive creature that is both resilient and charismatic and that represents our cultural and pastoral history." The conservation effort is supported by the County Mayo Foundation.

In the United States, dairy breeds were imported in the early 1900s. Those dams probably contained more biodiversity than goats in France and Switzerland do today, but, as modern American goats have been greatly improved for yield, the same loss of diversity will apply. Original genetic resources lie in Spanish and English (Arapawa) goats imported in the 16th and 17th centuries. The origin of San Clemente goats is unknown, but they represent a unique gene pool quite different from that found in dairy. These breeds are adapted to their local region and, if diversity is maintained in their gene pool, their descendants will be capable of adapting to changing conditions. These breeds are currently at risk, even critically endangered.

The FAO report is encouraging: more heritage breeds are being protected worldwide, but inbreeding and use of non-native breeds is still commonplace and a major cause of genetic erosion. Europe and North America have the highest proportion of at risk breeds.

Updated from article originally published as "Lessons from Cows" in the September/October 2017 issue of Dairy Goat Journal *and on countrysidenetwork.com.*

Sources:
Cassidy, L.M., et al. 2017. Capturing goats: documenting two hundred years of mitochondrial DNA diversity among goat populations from Britain and Ireland. *Biology Letters* 13: 20160876.

EU Horizon 2020: Saving animal DNA for future generations. Accessed March 17, 2018. https://ec.europa.eu/programmes/horizon2020/en/news/saving-animal-dna-future-generations.

FAO: Genetic diversity of livestock can help feed a hotter, harsher world. Accessed March 17, 2018. www.fao.org/news/story/en/item/380661/icode/.

Institut de l'Elevage IDELE: Diversité Génétique, des repères pour agir.

Oltenacu, P.A., and Broom, D.M., 2010. The impact of genetic selection for increased milk yield on the welfare of dairy cows. *Animal Welfare UFAW 2010*: 39–49.

Taberlet, P., et al. 2008. Are cattle, sheep, and goats endangered species? *Molecular Ecology* 17: 275–84.

Researchers and
Their Studies

Social Recognition ... and the Value of Research

Do your goats prick up their ears when they hear your voice? Do they respond to each other's bleats? They may hesitate when they spot you in the distance, but come running as soon as you call. My goats are shy of new people, so when helpers open their gate, they hold back. But I only need to call from around the corner for them to come running out to find me. They greet us and each other with a contact call that is both individual and stamped with a community accent.

Such individual recognition is important to highly social animals, as they form strong personal bonds and alliances, and navigate a competitive hierarchy. Does this sound like your goats? I'm sure that you, like me, have enjoyed watching their social interactions, how they form friends and challenge each other. However, husbandry guides and welfare standards don't yet advise how to take goat behavior into consideration when designing management systems. As goat farming becomes more popular and intensive, it is important that these facts are taken into account.

This is why researchers from Queen Mary University of London (QMUL), led by Alan McElligott, were investigating observations by goat keepers of how their animals behave. They have found that goats can learn a variety of complicated tasks by various means. Goats can learn a complicated food puzzle by trial and error. Goats can follow a route to feed demonstrated by a human. Goats look to human caregivers when they need help to access feed. Body posture and calls communicate their emotions, and bleats contain information on sex, age, size, group, and identity. They have long memories for individual recognition and how to complete a task.

Sounds pretty obvious to those of us who know goats well, don't you think? So what is the point of researchers spending time and money on such studies? Because legislation, welfare guidelines and agricultural training manuals will not incorporate advice on how to manage goats unless it is backed up by scientific evidence. To ensure good welfare, we need to train handlers well and provide an environment that suits goats' nature. Not only will this result in happier goats, but also in healthier animals that produce better and for longer. It is well known that stressed goats are more susceptible to disease and diminished production. McElligott found that most recommendations were based on studies of sheep, and he determined to bring about the necessary changes, as sheep and goats have quite different needs and personalities.

One piece of the puzzle in the scientific study of goat behavior came from a study by Benjamin Pitcher and the team from QMUL. Ten caprine residents at Buttercups Sanctuary for Goats, Kent, England, were tested to see if they can match a recording of a bleat to the goat who made it. Each "listener" goat faced two sample goats and was played sample bleats from a loudspeaker positioned between the two. When one of the sample goats was a pen-mate and the other a less familiar goat, the subject chose by staring at the correct goat quickly and for a long time in both cases. If the subject had two unfamiliar goats to choose from, the choice was delayed and glances were shorter. This suggests that the listener was clear who was bleating when a pen-mate was present, as the pen-mate's voice was familiar, and, by a process of elimination, the listener chose the unfamiliar goat when the bleat was not recognized. On the other hand, when faced with two less familiar goats and recordings of unknown bleats, the subject did not readily pick a goat to look at. This indicates both good memory for social information and logical reasoning in goats.

Slot this piece of evidence into the growing picture of goat social life and you see an intelligent being with strong friendships, long-term family ties, a complex social system and logical reasoning skills. Although, as keepers, we may already be aware of goat sensibilities, industry and consumers are unlikely to know this. To receive fair prices for our hard-earned products, we need to raise the profile of goat welfare, and ensure that the future of goats and goat farming is sustainable in a competitive marketplace.

Sources:

Alan McElligott. University of Roehampton, London. Accessed March 17, 2018. www.alanmcelligott.co.uk.

Pitcher, B.J., et al. 2017. Cross-modal recognition of familiar conspecifics in goats. *Royal Society Open Science* 4: 160346.

Goats are Skilled Observers

Goat watching is a hobby of mine! Once they get used to my presence and go back to browsing as normal, I can wonder at how attentive they are to possible dangers and feeding opportunities. I can observe how they browse selectively, moving to specific plants and fresher patches.

With progress in production and husbandry systems in mind, researchers study such behavior in our domestic goats. Foraging styles, social strategies, stress responses, the human–animal relationship, and the effects of different systems have all come under the empirical microscope. Intensification can lead to increased stress in goats. Some find it difficult to adapt to modern methods. They can get stressed by stock densities, systems that trigger flight reactions, fear of the unknown, or alarm at the unexpected. Therefore, it is important to understand how goats perceive their world, and that is where the study of farm animal cognition is concerned.

Jan Langbein of the Leibniz Institute for Farm Animal Biology, Dummerstorf, Germany, has been investigating the cognitive abilities of goats, among other farm animals, since 2002. In 2012 and 2013, he and Eberhard von Borell collaborated with PhD student Christian Nawroth, who was specializing in farm animal cognition.

Choose a cup, but not any cup!

Nawroth turned his attention to goats. He wanted to know whether they understood that food still existed when hidden, if they could work out where it was hidden, and if they could take directions from a person. In a specially designed stall, Nawroth taught ten Nigerian dwarf goats to come to a window for treats; each would poke their muzzle through a gap to take a snack from a cup. Clever design enabled these cups to conceal snacks without giving odor, or any other clues, and encouraged the goats to indicate which cup they believed contained food.

Out of sight, out of mind?

The goats watched Nawroth hide the food, and then were given a choice of cups to investigate. They mostly went for the cup with food hidden inside, demonstrating they realized the food was still there, although they could not see or smell it. This implies they understand hidden objects still exist. Recognizing this important stage in brain development helps us to gauge how a goat understands her environment, and we can take steps to make it less alarming and more interesting.

The cups and ball trick

What if Nawroth now moved the cups after food was hidden inside? He put a treat in only one cup and swapped their positions. If the cups were different in appearance, three of the goats were good at picking the correct cup. Tracking hidden objects is thought to help foraging goats keep track of the herd in deep vegetation.

The goats were also trained that the treat would normally be hidden under a certain cup, but most were not fooled by hiding it under a different one. This is another ability that is recognized as important in brain development.

Is your goat right-hoofed?

Understanding the inquisitive nature of goats and their acute senses, the researchers went to efforts to ensure they gave no unintentional clues to where the treats were hidden. They even had to redo some sessions if something they did had given them away. Strangely, they found that goats were better at picking the right cup if it was on their right-hand side and, unsurprisingly, if it were passed closer to them.

Goats that stare at men

The goats turned their attention to Nawroth—as they would, knowing he was a supplier of tasty treats. Interestingly, their behavior was markedly different depending on whether he was facing them or not. If he looked directly at them, even with his eyes closed, they anticipated a treat, pawing the partition and nosing at the window. If he looked away or turned his back, they stared attentively at him. It seems they were sensitive to the position of the human face, watching him while he was facing away, but only expecting treats when he faced them. Once he left the room their attention waned. This reminded me of my own goats, who stand to attention once they see or hear me, always hoping I'm bringing them something good.

Getting the point

This time Nawroth did not let the goats see where he had hidden the treat. He wanted to see if they would follow his directions to where it was hidden. He found most of them understood if he touched or pointed at the cups, some of them learning what pointing meant as the sessions progressed.
However, they did not understand that a person just looking at a cup was an indication of the location of food.

A different view

As you've noticed, goats' eyes are quite different from ours. The lateral pupil gives them a focused view at distance over a wide horizontal plane. I find it quite difficult to know exactly where my goats are focusing from looking at their eyes, as the spherical shape and lateral pupil take in so much. However, it is easy to see where their head is pointing. Previous studies had noted that goats follow the gaze of their herd mates, but, as we see here, they understand our eyeball direction no more than we do theirs.
However, they can learn to understand our pointing hands. They are also well aware of when we are paying them attention and when we are not.

Different skills for different lifestyles

Goats naturally browse in dry, mountainous conditions, and they know how to get the most out of a varied diet. This is thought to have improved their discriminatory and food finding skills, which is well demonstrated by these studies. This explains the high activity, playfulness, and perceived naughtiness of our beloved caprines. Now that goats live with us, we need to take these enhanced skills into consideration. We find that goats which have fun things to do are generally calmer and fight less. Researchers have investigated different environments and the effect of adding enriching activities. The results show that even adult goats that don't have access to free-ranging over large and varying areas benefit from having things to play with or climb on, such as planks, trunks, and hanging branches.

Pastures new

Following his PhD, Nawroth moved to England to continue studying behavior at Buttercups Goat Sanctuary with Queen Mary University of London. He joined a research team, headed by Alan McElligott, to observe willing subjects from among the sanctuary's approximately 140 residents. Nawroth continues to study the human–animal relationship, memory, decision-making, learning, and personality in goats.

Originally published in the July/August 2016 issue of Dairy Goat Journal *and on countrysidenetwork.com.*

Sources:

Kaminski, J., et al. 2005. Domestic goats, *Capra hircus*, follow gaze direction and use social cues in an object choice task. *Animal Behaviour* 69(1): 11–18.

Nawroth, C., von Borell, E., and Langbein, J. 2015. Goats that stare at men: dwarf goats alter their behaviour in response to human head orientation, but do not spontaneously use head direction as a cue in a food-related context. *Animal Cognition* 18(1): 65–73.

Nawroth, C., von Borell, E., and Langbein, J. 2015. Object permanence in the dwarf goat (*Capra aegagrus hircus*): Perseveration errors and the tracking of complex movements of hidden objects. *Applied Animal Behaviour Science* 167: 20–26.

Nawroth, C., von Borell, E., and Langbein, J. 2016. Goats that stare at men—revisited: Do dwarf goats alter their behaviour in response to eye visibility and head direction of a human? *Animal Cognition* 19(3): 667–72.

How Do Goats Think and Feel?

Have you ever wondered what your goats are thinking and how they feel about life? Such questions encouraged Elodie Briefer, a Swiss animal behavior researcher specializing in acoustic communication, to study goat cognition with Queen Mary University of London, England.

Having studied skylark song in Paris, Briefer wished to go on to study mammal calls with animals she could observe more closely. A colleague suggested she contact Alan McElligott in London. He wanted to study how goat mothers communicate with their kids to investigate the influence of behavior that evolved in the wild before domestication. McElligott had realized that most guidance on goat husbandry was based on sheep. Knowing, as any goat-keeper does, that goats are very different from their ovine relatives, he was keen to reveal evidence of their true nature. Scientific research is often based on what we already know about a species, because statutory guidelines and agricultural manuals do not include knowledge unless it is backed up by evidence. Briefer started her postdoctoral study with McElligott at a pygmy goat farm in Nottingham.

They studied contact calls between dams and their offspring. They found that mothers and kids recognized each other by voice by at least one week after birth, a skill that would help them to find each other when kids are hiding in the undergrowth of their ancestral lands. These natural skills have been retained by goats after some 10,000 years of domestication. Even in modern settings, kids seek places to hide out with their siblings while their mother is browsing, and feel safer when we provide them with such facilities.

On analyzing calls at different times, Briefer found that the age, sex, and body size of the kids affected their voices, and that the bleats of members of a group would gradually begin to resemble each other, even if the kids were not related, so that the group would form its own accent.

Even a year later, the mothers still reacted to recordings of their kids' calls, even if they had been separated after weaning. This gave Briefer and McElligott an indication of how good a long-term memory this species has. As Briefer says, "... we then both 'fell in love' with this species." They decided to continue studying goats and focus on their cognition and emotions, "... because they seemed very 'smart' to us, and not much was known about their intelligence."

Moving on to study a large herd of 150 rescued goats at Buttercups Sanctuary for Goats in Kent, England, Briefer was struck by the skills of two caprine residents. One old Saanen wether, Byron, could lock himself in his pen when he wanted to rest without disturbance from other herd members. Another wether, Ginger, would shut his pen gate behind him when he and the other goats came into the stable at night. However, when his stable-mate arrived, he would open the pen to let in his friend only, and then lock the gate behind them.

This clever ability to master latches encouraged the researchers to design tests that would produce evidence of goats' learning and manipulating skills. They built a treat-dispenser that required a lever to be pulled then lifted to release a piece of dried pasta. Nine out of ten goats tested learned to use the machine by trial and error within six days. They remembered how to do it after ten months, and again after two years, without further exposure to the equipment. Star pupil, Willow, a British Alpine doe, still remembered, with no hesitation at all, after four years.

However, watching a demonstrator use the equipment did not help them to learn the procedure quicker. They had to work it out for themselves. In another test, the QMUL team found that goats paid no heed to where another goat had found food and would readily explore other locations. These findings were unexpected, as goats are social animals, living in a herd. It was presumed that they learn from one another. Recent studies have certainly shown that kids learn from their mothers, and that tame goats will follow a route taken by a familiar human. This implies that, in the right circumstances, they use cues supplied by herd members. However, in these cases, where close up dexterity was required, and when the demonstrator goat had left the testing area, the goats relied on their own knowledge and learning abilities. These observations reflect the fact that goats originally adapted to difficult terrain, where food was scarce, so that each goat would have to search for the best forage.

Individual thinkers goats may be, but they share their emotions, mainly through body language. Briefer and her team measured the intensity of goat emotional states and whether they are positive or negative. Their aim was to establish easy, non-invasive assessment methods. Intense emotions induce faster breathing, increased movement and bleating; calls are higher pitched and ears are alert and pointed forward. Positive states are displayed by a lifted tail and a steady voice, while negative ones are characterized by ears flicked back and a shaky bleat.

Longer-term moods may reflect a goat's outlook on her environment and treatment. The goat sanctuary was the perfect place to compare goats that had been neglected or poorly treated before being rescued with those that had always been well cared for. Goats that had been at the sanctuary for more than two years were tested for cognitive bias. This is a test to gauge an individual's view of the world: optimistic or pessimistic. Is the bowl half empty or half full? In this case, a bucket containing feed was placed at the end of a corridor. Goats were allowed access to two corridors, one at a time, and learned that one contained feed, while the other was empty. Once they had learned this, the goats were much quicker to enter the stocked corridor than the empty one. Goats were then given access to intermediate corridors, placed between two. What would goats expect of a bucket in an unknown corridor? Would they envisage it to be empty or full? Would goats that had suffered poor welfare be less hopeful? In fact, within males no difference in optimism was seen, whereas females with bad pasts were more optimistic than does with a stable background. The beneficial effects of the sanctuary had no doubt enabled these resilient does to bounce back and recover.

After six years of study, Briefer concludes that goats are intelligent, emotional, stubborn, and have a mind of their own. She thinks they'd make good pets if they didn't insist on escaping and eating trees, vegetables, flowers, and even your notebook. They should be respected and treated in line with their emotional and cognitive abilities in order to improve their living conditions. She says, "... their intelligence has been ignored for so long, and our research allows [us] to highlight the fact that they possess good cognitive abilities and their housing should be adapted to these abilities. I find that very exciting. Finally, the indicators of emotions that we found could be used to assess their welfare."

Originally published in the May/June 2017 issue of Dairy Goat Journal *and on countrysidenetwork.com.*

Sources:

Briefer, E. 2016. A quoi pensent les chèvres? In Matignon, K.L. 2016. *Révolutions animales: comment les animaux sont devenus intelligents,* pp. 54–58.

Briefer, E., and McElligott, A.G. 2011. Indicators of age, body size and sex in goat kid calls revealed using the source–filter theory. *Applied Animal Behaviour Science* 133(3–4): 175–85.

Briefer, E., and McElligott, A.G. 2011. Mutual mother–offspring vocal recognition in an ungulate hider species (Capra hircus). *Animal Cognition*: 14(4): 585–98.

Briefer, E.F., et al. 2014. Goats excel at learning and remembering a highly novel cognitive task. *Frontiers in Zoology* 11: 20.

Briefer, E.F., and McElligott, A.G. 2013. Rescued goats at a sanctuary display positive mood after former neglect. *Applied Animal Behaviour Science* 146(1–4): 45–55.

Briefer, E.F., and McElligott, A.G. 2012. Social effects on vocal ontogeny in an ungulate, the goat, Capra hircus. *Animal Behaviour* 83(4): 991–1000.

Briefer, E.F., Oxley, J.A., and McElligott, A.G. 2015. Autonomic nervous system reactivity in a free-ranging mammal: effects of dominance rank and personality. *Animal Behaviour* 110: 121–32.

Briefer, E.F., Tettamanti, F., and McElligott, A.G. 2015. Emotions in goats: mapping physiological, behavioural and vocal profiles. *Animal Behaviour* 99: 131–43.

Briefer, E.F., de la Torre, M.P., and McElligott, A.G. 2012. Mother goats do not forget their kids' calls. *Proceedings of the Royal Society of London B: Biological Sciences* 279(1743): 3749–55.

Brain Training for Happy Goats

Domestication has worked over 10,000 years to transform the goat from its wild ancestor, the Bezoar, into the farmyard friend we know today. Selective breeding brings about obvious changes in size, conformation, and yield. Additional physical and behavioral changes accompany selection for any specific trait, and these are sometimes quite unexpected. For example, breeding for a calm and friendly temperament in silver foxes also resulted in floppier ears, curlier tails and coat color changes. Similarly, breeding for productivity may result in behavior changes in goats.

We may soon know how domestication has affected the goat mind. Researchers at the Leibniz Institute for Farm Animal Biology (FBN), Germany, and Agroscope, Switzerland, started a three-year project in 2017 investigating and comparing the cognition and learning abilities of modern domestic and wild goats. As Birger Puppe, manager of the FBN Institute of Behavioral Physiology, explains, "Cognition tests are an important tool in the comparative study of learning and cognitive performance of wild and domesticated animals. Corresponding changes in behavior can only be investigated in a few animal species, since the presence of the wild ancestor of domesticated species is a prerequisite for this."

These studies are not funded simply to satisfy academic curiosity, but are seen as a crucial steppingstone towards the future sustainability of farming practices. Animal welfare is vital to healthy production. In order to maintain good living conditions while production demands increase, we need an understanding of how farm animals perceive the world that we are building for them. Agricultural environments often restrict natural behavior and can lead to boredom, frustration, and stress, especially in a highly active species like the goat. The provision of stimulating activity has already shown positive effects in captive animals. "An in-depth understanding of the cognitive abilities and demands of farm animals is a prerequisite for more suitable husbandry conditions in the future, taking into account appropriate cognitive challenges, as has long been realized with zoo animals," emphasized project manager Jan Langbein.

Operant conditioning is training by rewarding specific behaviors, for example, through clicker training. It is believed to improve well-being by allowing an animal to control aspects of its environment. Focusing on a rewarding task brings the satisfaction of achievement and confidence to cope with challenges. In addition, the design of appropriate housing and husbandry equipment needs to consider the perspective of the animal mind that will experience it. Rapid development of production techniques may be encouraging management changes, and goats have so far proved their adaptability. However, we must be careful not to push our animals beyond the limits of their coping abilities.

Simulating the wild environment may not be the answer. Goats' long history of domestication has changed their needs beyond those of their wild ancestors, as they have adapted to living with us. When we breed goats, we naturally pick those that do well in captivity with the resources we can provide. We also favor those that are easy to handle and that produce well in our care. In recent years we have focused specifically on certain traits, creating breeds for different functions. These changes may have a knock-on effect on the personality and intellect of the goat. Dairy goats may react to life differently than meat goats and from their ancestors. For this reason, the researchers plan to study and compare a dairy herd in Switzerland and Nigerian dwarfs in Germany, breeds originally developed towards different ends, as well as a wild relative. "The value of the results can increase significantly, by repeating the tests at two research sites under comparable husbandry conditions," said Langbein.

Goats are descended from a wild goat, the Bezoar, first domesticated approximately 10,000 years ago in Anatolia and the Zagros Mountains in the Middle East. During the late Neolithic period, just before 6000 BC, when agriculture was spreading over Asia and Europe, early domesticated Bezoar were brought to Crete as utility animals. They subsequently turned feral and now live wild in the Samaria Gorge of the White Mountains. Now known as kri-kri, the Cretan wild goat, they are the emblem of this Greek island, symbolic in historic and touristic literature. Only found around Crete or in zoos, they bear little mark of their early domestication and are believed to closely resemble their wild ancestor, which they share with the goat.

The researchers are studying a major population of kri-kri at Dählhölzli Animal Park, Berne, Switzerland. This herd, as well as the two domesticated ones, receive rewarding cognitive training. The team measure their abilities and learning styles, and observe the effects of training on their well-being and ability to deal with challenges. Results are expected by 2019.

FBN have been studying farm animal behavior for 15 years and have been influential in dispelling the myth prevalent in Germany that goats are stupid. They have shown that goats are adept at associating a complex computer-generated symbol with a reward and picking out the correct symbol from four choices. Goats can learn and remember correct symbols from several sets, and learning one puzzle helps them to solve further puzzles faster. They can work out a general pattern, such as discovering that all hollow symbols of any shape are the key to the prize. But do they enjoy doing this? Preliminary studies suggest that they do.

An increased heart rate can indicate excitement or stress, whereas increased heart rate variability occurs on relaxation. When goats first attempted to operate the puzzle, they had a period of frustration, not understanding how it worked, which was reflected in a depressed heart rate. As they started to get results, heart rate went up, suggesting a lift in mood and excitement. As they mastered the tasks, heart rate variability improved as relaxation kicked in. It appeared that the confidence and interest elicited by learning was good for the heart! But how did it affect their ability to cope? A study of physical and cognitive enrichment compared the behavior of goats living with climbing apparatus to those with a computerized learning device and to those with both or none. When these goats were presented with a challenge that might frighten most goats—being alone in a strange pen with an unfamiliar object—those from the enriched pens were much more proactive and inquisitive. Goats that used climbing apparatus were more active and made more effort to rejoin their herd. Those who used the learning device were more curious about the strange object and investigated it for longer. The physical exercise afforded by the climbing frame was also seen to improve mental learning abilities.

Enrichment appears to improve the animals' competence and reduce boredom. The beauty of the learning device is that it can be regularly changed to present new puzzles, so the novelty does not wear off as easily as it does with physical toys. But do the goats still choose to solve the puzzle when they can get the same reward for free? Another study revealed that this depends very much on the ability of the individual, with high achievers often preferring the learning device. On average, a third of all goats' interactions were still directed at the learning device when a free dispenser was available.

Learning could prove to be an important tool for ensuring the welfare of our goats, making sure that they do not get bored and helping them to deal with stress. Understanding how they see the world will help us to design equipment and housing with their welfare in mind.

Originally published in the July/August 2017 issue of Dairy Goat Journal *and on countrysidenetwork.com.*

Sources:

Animal Health and Animal Welfare (in German). Leibniz Institute for Farm Animal Biology (FBN). Accessed March 17, 2018. www.fbn-dummerstorf.de.

Bar-Gal, G.K., et al. 2002. Genetic evidence for the origin of the agrimi goat (*Capra aegagrus cretica*). *Journal of Zoology 256*(3): 369–77.

Langbein, J., Nürnberg, G., and Manteuffel, G. 2004. Visual discrimination learning in dwarf goats and associated changes in heart rate and heart rate variability. *Physiology & Behavior* 82: 601–09.

Langbein, J., Siebert, K., and Nürnberg, G. 2009. On the use of an automated learning device by group-housed dwarf goats: Do goats seek cognitive challenges? *Applied Animal Behaviour Science* 120: 150–58.

Oesterwind, S., et al. 2016. Impact of structural and cognitive enrichment on the learning performance, behavior and physiology of dwarf goats (*Capra aegagrus hircus*). *Applied Animal Behaviour Science* 177: 34–41.

Goat Behavior Takes the Podium: A Summary of Research in 2016

Goats featured in five presentations at 2016's Congress of the International Society for Applied Ethology on July 12–16, in Edinburgh, Scotland. The Society meets annually to discuss researchers' discoveries about domestic animal behavior and welfare.

Scottish and French researchers teamed up to study how goats perceive the facial expressions of their caprine companions. Lucille Bellegarde of INRA, France, while studying her PhD at SRUC, Scotland, presented her team's findings of goats' reactions to photographs of their herd mates in a negative and a positive situation. Goats were photographed while being groomed and also while having an icepack applied to their udders. No prizes for guessing which treatment the goats preferred! Goats experiencing an unpleasant situation rotate their ears backwards and show tension in their nostrils and jaw muscles. On the other hand, goats voluntarily being groomed (meaning the goat must initiate or stand without restraint for the treatment) have relaxed facial muscles and droop their ears horizontally.

Companions of the photographed goats were shown these kinds of image on a computer screen, and recordings revealed that goats were more alert to photographs of negative expressions than those of relaxed goats. This may be due to a goat's need to be aware of any dangerous situation that may threaten the herd. The data also revealed that the goats showed more interest in some of their companions than others, perhaps due to their position in the hierarchy.

The relaxing effect of voluntary grooming by humans has been a subject of study by Queen Mary University of London (QMUL). Elodie Briefer and her team's paper on the effect on the goats' nervous system was published in December 2015. Goats were found to be most relaxed during voluntary grooming sessions, even more than when resting. However, feeding was found to be even more exciting than combat. More social goats were found to have less reactive heart rates.

Briefer had previously analyzed bleats and found that positive ones tended to be more stable in pitch. You can tell if your goat is having a negative experience if you hear her making a shaky bleat. The more stressed or excited a goat is, the louder and higher pitched her call will be. By communicating emotion through their bleats, goats remain alert to warnings from herd members, and react quickly to any potential danger. The emotional contagion can spread quickly through the herd and put the whole group on edge. It is important to understand such effects when managing livestock, so that animals do not become over-stressed.

Gentle and quiet handling by a sympathetic stock-person has been shown to calm feral goats captured for the feedlot in Australia. David Miller of Murdoch University presented his team's findings of reduced antagonism and fear in penned feral goats that had regular exposure to a friendly person compared to those with little human contact.

Goats will follow a human friend who is demonstrating how to access a food source, as QMUL's Christian Nawroth explained to the congress. Goats shown the correct path to the food learned quicker than those who had no such demonstration. After many studies with eager subjects from Buttercups Sanctuary for Goats, Nadia and her herd mates have no qualms about following their favorite researchers!

The process for publishing scientific results takes time due to scrupulous reviews and revisions. However, 2016 saw several goat studies published in respected scientific journals and worldwide in the popular press. You may remember reports of Nadia from Buttercups Sanctuary for Goats showing the world how goats look to humans for assistance, just like dogs do. When Nadia found she could not open a clear box containing treats, she approached a person who was looking her way and looked at him in the face, even pawing him for assistance. She did not request attention from other researchers who were looking away. Several other goats at the sanctuary displayed similar behavior.

Nadia and her herd-mates also featured in a study of how personality affects learning in goats. Researchers noted goats' reactions to isolation or reintroduction to their pen-mates and their responses to new objects and environments. They classified their personalities according to how sociable or inquisitive they were. The goats then were given treats when they resolved puzzles and their personality and quiz scores were compared. One test was to find which cup contained a hidden treat after transposing the cups. The other was to guess whether a black or white cup contained the secret snack, after being trained to eat from a container of one or other color. Less explorative goats performed better in the transposition test and less sociable goats performed better at choosing the correct color. It could be that the less active goats are more observant, and sociable goats depend more on learning from others than figuring it out for themselves. A further test ensured that the animals did not have learning deficiencies. It revealed that some goats preferred to use visual clues, while others focused more on the location of previous treats. The tests hint that varying personality traits may equip goats with different skills for dealing with their environment.

Originally published in the November/December 2016 issue of Dairy Goat Journal *and on countrysidenetwork.com.*

Sources:

Bellegarde, L.G.A., et al. 2017. Face-based perception of emotions in dairy goats. *Applied Animal Behaviour Science* 193: 51–59.

Briefer, E.F., Oxley, J.A., and McElligott, A.G. 2015. Autonomic nervous system reactivity in a free-ranging mammal: effects of dominance rank and personality. *Animal Behaviour* 110: 121–32.

Briefer, E.F., Tettamanti, F., and McElligott, A.G. 2015. Emotions in goats: mapping physiological, behavioural and vocal profiles. *Animal Behaviour* 99: 131–43.

Dwyer C., Haskell, M., and Sandilands, V. ISAE 2016: *Proceedings of the 50th congress of the International Society for Applied Ethology, 12–15 July, 2016,* Edinburgh, United Kingdom: standing on the shoulders of giants. pp. 175, 178, 182, 193, and 401.

Miller, D.W., et al. 2018. Behavioural assessment of the habituation of feral rangeland goats to an intensive farming system. *Applied Animal Behaviour Science* 199: 1–8.

Nawroth, C., Baciadonna, L., and McElligott, A.G. 2016. Goats learn socially from humans in a spatial problem-solving task. *Animal Behaviour* 121: 123–29.

Nawroth, C., Brett, J.M., and McElligott, A.G. 2016. Goats display audience-dependent human-directed gazing behaviour in a problem-solving task. *Biology Letters* 12(7): 20160283.

Nawroth, C., Prentice, P.M., and McElligott, A.G. 2016. Individual personality differences in goats predict their performance in visual learning and non-associative cognitive tasks. *Behavioural Processes* 134: 43–53.

Reading Goats' Minds: A Summary of Research in 2017

We've had to learn to be smart, to stay one step ahead of probing muzzles and fiddling lips that find their way into food bins or out of pens. We, their handlers, know how smart goats are. But do we think goat-wise, understanding caprine minds: how they see their environment and us, how they learn, how learning can affect their future experience, and how their experience affects their health and production? To this end, researchers continue to delve into the minds of goats, to gauge how goats are affected by the production environment and their interactions with people.

In 2017, we saw published results of studies into cognition, human–goat relationships, reproductive behavior, and reaction to intensive conditions. Knowledge of the goats' perspective enables us to design goat-friendly accommodation and tailor our procedures and handling techniques to reduce stress. Enjoyable, stress-free living will optimize the health and production of our animals—and benefit us too!

What matters to goats

We know that goats are curious and quickly learn the best way to get treats. We've heard that they have long memories. This year, researchers in London, England, described how individuals differ in their understanding of the world. Some seek food in places where they've been successful before, while others go by the color or shape of food containers. Some learn more by investigating and others by watching. These personal differences have been found to be linked to personality types. Less sociable goats were better at finding food hidden in cups of different colors, perhaps because they worried less about their absent pen-mates. These goats tended to use shape and color of feed bowl to locate treats, rather than rely on bowl position. Goats that explore less are better at tracking hidden objects when they are moved, possibly due to their calm, observational manner.

Goats have shown that they can learn unusual tasks, even choosing abstract symbols to request a drink of water at the German research center. They can even restrain their natural urge to go for food seen through a barrier after learning the correct route to access the treat. Even so, many goats still let their belly rule their head!

Goats may appear to have one-track minds, but they devote a lot of thought to social issues too. London researchers found that goats recognized the voices of their close friends and looked at their pen-mate when they heard the sound of their bleat. If there is a less familiar goat present when they heard an unknown bleat, they looked at the lesser-known individual, showing that they inferred this goat had made the call.

They are sensitive to herd-mates' facial expressions. French goats paid more attention when they saw the photographed face of a familiar goat in an unpleasant situation than when they saw that of a relaxed, contented companion. They also paid more attention to certain individuals' pictures, and Alpines looked more at the photographs than Saanens.

As a group, goats benefit from behaving unpredictably, so they can outsmart predators—and us! A London herd were found to have no predominant preference overall for starting out with their left or right foot forwards, although some individuals showed a left- or right-hoofed tendency.

Scent is an important social signal for goats, especially during the breeding season. Buck scent is attractive to does, and has been found to encourage male virility by New Jersey researchers. By urinating on his beard and face, a buck increases his own testosterone levels as well as enticing females. A Mexican team studying reproduction found an active buck can even encourage does to perform sexual displays out of season, whether they have had previous sexual experience or not.

Kids need mother's milk, but dams too have their needs: adequate nutrition and a release from the physical drain of feeding growing young. As newborns naturally hide, it had been thought that they may feed less during the first week. However, Mexican researchers found that kids penned with their dam suckled most during the first week, when their dam rarely prevented them. After two weeks, dams increasingly rejected or interrupted suckling sessions, marking the start of a very gradual weaning process. Previous studies had shown that kids' eagerness ensured them a steady milk supply, and natural weaning began in earnest at six to seven weeks old, as kids' intake of solid food increased. Contact between dam and kids helped to maintain a high milk production, and early separation can have the effect of reducing yield.

What goats think of us

In 2017, there was a focus on how goats interpret human appearance and behavior, and how they interact with us. Handling is an important part of stress management and can make all the difference when we are obliged to carry out procedures such as healthcare and transportation.

We've seen how goats learn new tricks by doing what we do, and this has been replicated in a scientific environment by researchers in London. Goats learned quicker to go around a barrier to get to food after watching a human do it.

The same team demonstrated how goats came to a human observer for help accessing a treat in a closed container. The goats consistently chose humans who were watching rather than others who were looking away. This observation gave rise to a series of trials to ascertain how goats chose a human assistant. Goats approach humans from the front when they want our attention, but are not concerned whether the human is looking away. This might be because goats have lateral eyes and can see well to the side as well as the front. They probably don't realize that we have poor peripheral vision. They prefer to approach a human whose eyes are open and whose head is not obscured, so appear to realize our requirements to see. However, a partially obscured face did not deter them, and the location of hands did not influence them. It seems they aim to gain our visual attention rather than going straight to our hands to check for treats.

Knowing how goats see us should help us to communicate effectively with them, which allows us to manage them smoothly.

How goats react to management systems

Just a subtle change in human behavior can affect goats in ways that we may not envisage, unless we think goat-wise. This may affect goats in confined systems even more than those at range: firstly, because they may have less regular contact with humans, and secondly because they are less able to run from stressful situations.

Feral goats are initially frightened of human contact, an issue for Australian feral goats moving into production systems. Groups where a human walked calmly among them twice a day showed a marked reduction in fear of humans, less aggression between herd members, and were generally calmer after three weeks compared to those with little human interaction.

Several studies have already addressed the effect of confinement, sterile environments, and lack of space on goat behavior, and how to alleviate stress through good housing design and social conditions. Swiss ruminant housing specialists recommend feeding shelves should be raised at least 10 cm (4 inches) from the level of the front hooves to allow comfortable access. This corresponds well to goats' natural grazing height and should avoid goats kneeling to feed. An Indian study of kids in different pen sizes confirms that larger stalls allow more comfort and healthy activity and reduce fighting. Mexican kids in enriched stalls showed fewer signs of stress.

In New Zealand, goats were found to prefer different kinds of bedding for different tasks: They preferred to lie down on plastic or rubber, warm, dry but firm surface rather than on metal or wood shavings; but preferred to use wood shavings as a toileting area. Surface use may also vary due to temperature, so researchers conclude that a choice of multiple surfaces can meet goats' needs.

Pain management studies have shown that routine procedures such as disbudding and elastration cause pain. An FAO study noted that increased head shaking and rubbing after disbudding is indicative of a painful experience. Such behavioral signs are important to note as ruminants normally hide their pain as a survival strategy.

Studies will continue to investigate how mental and physical comfort can be achieved in indoor and outdoor systems, as happy goats means a healthy and productive herd.

Updated from an article originally published in the November/December 2017 issue of Goat Journal *and on countrysidenetwork.com.*

Sources:

Baruzzi, C., et al. 2017. Motor asymmetry in goats during a stepping task. *Laterality: Asymmetries of Body, Brain and Cognition* 19: 1–11.

Bellegarde, L.G., et al. 2017. Face-based perception of emotions in dairy goats. *Applied Animal Behaviour Science* 193: 51–59.

Fritz, W.F., Becker, S.E., and Katz, L.S. 2017. Effects of simulated self-enurination on reproductive behavior and endocrinology during the transition into the breeding season in male goats. *Journal of Animal Science 95*(Supp 4): 4.

García y González, E., et al. 2017. Early nursing behaviour in ungulate mothers with hider offspring (Capra hircus): Correlations between milk yield and kid weight. *Small Ruminant Research* 151: 59–65.

Hempstead, M.N., et al. 2017. Behavioural response of dairy goat kids to cautery disbudding. *Applied Animal Behaviour Science* 194: 42–47.

Keil, N.M., et al. 2017. Determining suitable dimensions for dairy goat feeding places by evaluating body posture and feeding reach. *Journal of Dairy Science*: 100(2): 1353–62.

Langbein, J. 2017. Motor self-regulation by goats (*Capra aegagrus hircus*) in a detour-reaching task. Presentation at the 51st Congress of the International Society for Applied Ethology: Understanding Animal Behaviour, August 9, 2017.

Loya-Carrera, J.A., et al. 2017. Sexually inexperienced anestrous goats are able to exhibit sexual behaviors exposed to sexually active bucks. *JABB-Online Submission System* 5(2): 64–71.

Miller, D.W., et al. 2017. Behavioural assessment of the habituation of feral rangeland goats to an intensive farming system. *Applied Animal Behaviour Science* 199: 1–8.

Nawroth, C. 2017. Invited review: Socio-cognitive capacities of goats and their impact on human-animal interactions. *Small Ruminant Research* 150: 70–75.

Nawroth, C., Prentice, P.M., and McElligott, A.G. 2017. Individual personality differences in goats predict their performance in visual learning and non-associative cognitive tasks. *Behavioural Processes* 134: 43–53.

Nawroth, C., and McElligott, A.G. 2017. Human head orientation and eye visibility as indicators of attention for goats (Capra hircus). *Peer J*: e3073.

Pitcher, B.J., et al. 2017. Cross-modal recognition of familiar conspecifics in goats. *Open Science* 4(2): 160346.

Rosas-Trigueros, A.P., et al. 2017. Histological differences in the adrenal glands and cortisol levels of suckling dairy goat kids in enriched and non-enriched environments. *Research in Veterinary Science* 115: 221–25.

Sutherland, M.A., et al. 2017. Dairy goats prefer to use different flooring types to perform different behaviours. *Applied Animal Behaviour Science* 197: 24–31.

Thakur, A., et al. 2017. Effect of different floor space allowances on the performance and behavior of Beetal kids under stall-fed conditions. *Indian Journal of Animal Research* 51(4): 776–80.

Printed in Great Britain
by Amazon